THE PIG WAR

HOW A PORCINE TRAGEDY TAUGHT ENGLAND AND AMERICA TO SHARE

Emma Bland Smith   Illustrated by **Alison Jay**

CALKINS CREEK
AN IMPRINT OF ASTRA BOOKS FOR YOUNG READERS
New York

This is a true tale about two mighty nations, an ill-fated pig, and a most unusual war. It is also a story about sharing.

THE DATE: June 15, 1859.

THE SETTING: A small but lovely island called San Juan, off the green coast of today's Pacific Northwest. Was the island American? Was it British? That depended on who you asked.

THE CHARACTERS: A few dozen men who had gotten along okay, for the most part, for some years. What were they doing there? Well, the Brits were raising sheep for a powerful British corporation called the Hudson's Bay Company. The Americans? Most of them were former miners, looking for a bit of land to settle down on.

THE MOOD: About to change, for the worse.

On this spring day, an American settler named Lyman Cutlar looked out his window and spied a large pig rooting in his potato patch.
The pig was British. Or at least its owner was.

Now, the Brits and the Yanks were on fairly good terms. True, they'd fought a terrible war, America's War of Independence, nearly a century before. And then about thirty years later they'd clashed again, in the War of 1812. But since then things had calmed down. They were, if not exactly friends, then at least polite rivals in the exploration and settlement of the West.

But still, tempers can flare. And on this fateful morning, Lyman's did.

Maybe Lyman hadn't had his coffee. Maybe he'd slept poorly. Maybe he was looking forward to boiling those potatoes for his supper. Maybe he was thinking of the many painful miles he'd rowed to buy the potato seed. But for whatever reason, when he saw that pig, he got cranky.

He acted without thinking. And the pig paid the ultimate price.

Poor pig. Instantly, Lyman regretted his rashness. He hurried to the pig's owner, Charles Griffin, and offered to pay for the animal.

A gleam in his eye, Charles asked Lyman for a hundred dollars, and all would be forgiven.
Simple, right?
Not quite.

One hundred dollars was an outrageous sum at the time. For that kind of money, a person could buy a nice plot of land. A farm laborer earned only about two hundred dollars—*per year!*

Lyman refused to pay. "There is a better chance for lightning to strike you than for you to get a hundred dollars for that hog!" he said.

Charles was affronted. "You Americans are a nuisance on the island!" he bellowed. (In Charles's eyes, the island was British.)

"I consider it American soil!" retorted Lyman.

That was too much for Charles. By this time he was more than a little cranky himself. He told an official, who threatened to have Lyman arrested and all his fellow Americans evicted from the island.

The same day, Charles sat down and wrote
to his boss, James Douglas, the governor of the
Crown Colonies of Vancouver Island and British
Columbia. That should do it, he figured.

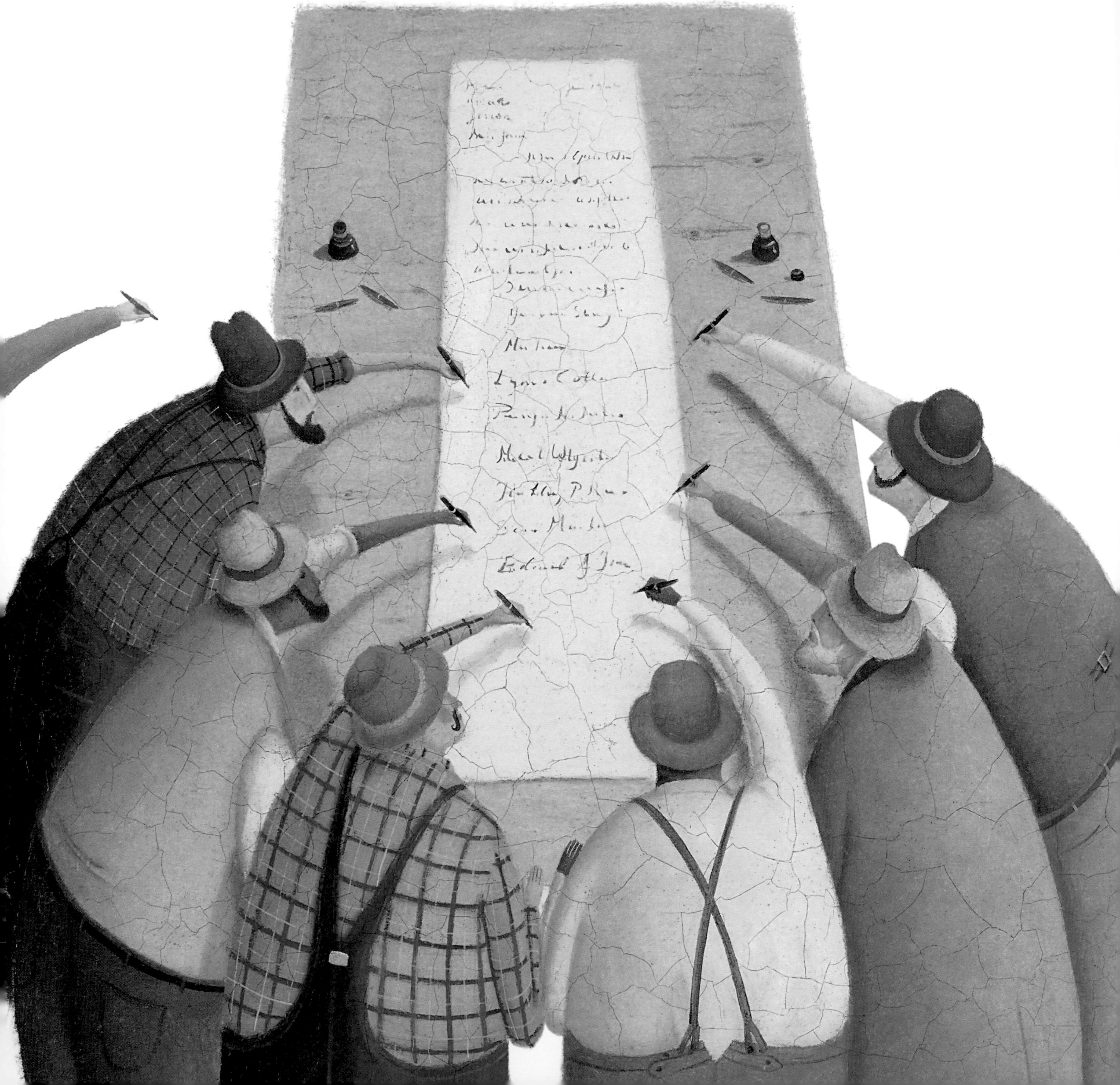

But those Yanks, they knew their way around a fountain pen, too. They wrote a letter to General William Harney, the American military commander, and signed it, all eighteen of them.

Now, the two bosses, Harney and Douglas, may or may not have been cranky. We don't know. But we do know that they were both—it must be said—on the hotheaded side. Harney promptly dispatched a company of sixty-four men, under the command of Captain George Pickett. The Americans must have sighed a breath of relief. Such a fearsome display of power would surely make the Brits back off.

Simple, right?

Not quite.

Because just two days later, a British ship, highly armed, commanded by Captain Geoffrey Hornby and loaded with several hundred men, steamed into the bay.

Oh, dear.
What started as a Pig Incident and turned into a Pig Argument was fast escalating into a Pig Situation.

Pickett was nervous. (Well, who wouldn't be?) He was also, like his boss, a bit of a hothead. He asked for reinforcements, and hundreds more American troops joined Pickett's forces on the island.

Hornby, though less of a hothead than *his* boss, the governor, likely felt a tad nervous himself at this point. Two more British ships steamed in. Soon the bay and the golden hills overlooking it teemed with British and American ships and soldiers, all on alert.

From shore, building a fort for their cannons, the Americans recalled the last two wars they'd fought with Britain. So many young men killed, so many children orphaned. Did they want to suffer that tragedy again?

From their ships, aiming their own cannons (they had sixty-four in all!), the British pondered their tentative relationship with the United States. Did they want to reignite the hostile attitudes of the past?

Both sides waited, anxious, wondering if a scuffle over a pig had gotten just a tad out of hand.

The Pig War was about to begin.

Tense days passed. The British captain, Hornby, taking a
risk, ignored the governor's orders to land marines on shore.
(Brave fellow!)

Then, unsure what to do next, Hornby waited for his superior, Rear Admiral R. Lambert Baynes. (Another good move!) Baynes was even less trigger-happy than Hornby. When he arrived and heard about the situation, he exclaimed (or so they say), "Tut, tut, no, no." Then he ordered his troops to sit tight, and added, in so many words, "Hold your fire!"

(Phew.)

On the American side, Lieutenant Colonel Silas Casey took over from Pickett. He, too, was admirably lacking in hotheadedness. He rowed out to one of the British ships and tried to talk things through. But still, neither side would back down.

By this time, the government bigwigs had heard what was happening. A squabble over a pig in a potato patch was about to plunge the two nations into war!

President James Buchanan, far off in Washington, D.C., was alarmed. So were the British officials. Buchanan sent a message. "Don't shoot—unless they shoot first!" was the order. (But in much fancier language.)

And with the approval of the Brits, the president dispatched a proven negotiator.

Hastily (or as hastily as possible for a time when it took six weeks to cross the country), General Winfield Scott arrived to help the two sides work things out. General Scott, it will not be disputed, was the least hotheaded of the whole gang. He worked his magic.

Maybe the soldiers missed their families. Maybe both sides had cooled off. Maybe General Scott was a persuasive speaker. Maybe all of the above. For whatever reason, the men put down their weapons. And the islanders agreed to share.

"Joint occupation," the officials called it. Following the agreement, most of the soldiers left. All but one of the warships sailed back out of the harbor. No more than one hundred men on each side were allowed to remain.

None of the artillery guns were ever fired—except one. On a landmark day in November 1859, as General Scott prepared to leave after negotiating for peace, the Americans gave him a one-gun salute. Well-deserved.

And now it was time to share.
Simple, right?
Actually, this time, quite right.

The residents established two bases—American Camp and English Camp. Together, they improved the island. They fixed the roads. They set up a bi-national patrol to keep order.

They even attended each other's holidays. Every summer the Americans celebrated the Fourth of July and invited the British. Every May 24 the British threw a birthday bash for their queen, Victoria, and the Americans always joined in. (The raucous games included horse racing, blindfolded wheelbarrow races, and balancing on a greased pole off the end of a ship. They knew how to have fun!)

Did Lyman participate in these good times? Probably—he was known as a fun-loving guy. Did he feel just a teensy bit embarrassed about all the fuss he'd caused? Let's hope so, for goodness' sake.

Today, San Juan is part of the United States.
English Camp and American Camp are still there,
flags waving, a reminder of the past.

The island, it is true, is small.

But what happened there was very, very big.
Two countries worked hard to share, to look past
their differences, and to get along. They did all
that—and no one got hurt.

Except the pig.

AUTHOR'S NOTE

I traveled to San Juan Island during the summer of 2017. I stood on the same prairie where the Pig War took place, overlooking the silver waters of the Salish Sea. I strolled the wild and beautiful American Camp, the quaint and tidy English Camp. Because the sites have been so wonderfully preserved and restored, I could easily picture myself back in 1859, when Lyman Cutlar shot that poor pig. From the moment I first read about the Pig War, I knew that what happened at San Juan was truly astonishing, and that feeling was compounded by my visit. They say that only by learning from the past can we progress and change. Revisiting this snippet of history has the potential to affect our future in a hugely positive way.

Was there really something called the Pig War? Yes indeed, although it was more of a cold war or a standoff, since no one died but the pig. The clash is remembered by historians as a unique example of two nations resolving a conflict without resorting to violence. The sites of the old American Camp and English Camp were turned into a national historical park in 1966, to honor the legacy of this remarkable event.

In the year 1846, the northwestern part of today's United States was still the Wild West. Various countries had claimed ownership of this area over the centuries (stubbornly ignoring the fact that the indigenous Coast Salish and Northwest Coast peoples had lived there much longer). The Spanish had explored and claimed it in the 1700s but dropped out by 1795, leaving it to the British. After the American Revolution, Britain had yielded much of today's United States (primarily all the land east of the Appalachians) to the Americans. But here in this northwestern corner the borders remained fuzzy, and the Americans and British, both still land-hungry, were eager to decide who owned what.

So the governments hammered out an agreement called the Oregon Treaty to determine ownership of the "Oregon Country" (or, as the British called it, "Columbia District." The Americans and the British even had different names for it!). The territory in question included what we now know as the states of Washington, Oregon, and Idaho, parts of Wyoming and Montana, and part of the Canadian province of British Columbia.

They essentially drew a line that started at the Rocky Mountains and headed west along the 49th parallel, which is now the U.S.-Canada border. Everything above the line would go to Britain (later becoming Canada), and everything below it would go to the United States.

Simple, right?

Not quite.

As the line approached the Pacific Ocean, near Seattle and Vancouver, the Oregon Treaty specified that the border should progress south through the channel that divided Vancouver Island from the mainland, then out the Strait of Juan de Fuca to the Pacific Ocean. The problem was, there were actually two channels, with San Juan and its sister islands between them. Would San Juan go to the British or to the Americans?

This was not an easy decision, and for good reason. People were quite taken with the island. One visitor called it "exquisitely beautiful"; another, "a paradise." Its grasslands were ideal for grazing sheep. The waters were brimming with salmon, cod, and halibut, and the land provided coal and limestone. Perhaps more significantly, both nations considered San Juan a potential political and military foothold on this part of the continent. Neither the Americans nor the British wanted to give it up. Not one bit.

Clearly, negotiation was called for—lengthy, possibly painful negotiation. But the two countries were impatient. In their haste to be done with the treaty, they decided . . . to put off the decision for later. (Procrastination. It happens to the best of us.)

And so nothing was decided. The British established first a salmon-salting station and then a successful sheep business on San Juan. American settlers (often failed or retired miners) heard about the island and claimed small farms there. (The Brits called them squatters.) There were small clashes and disagreements, and by that fateful day in 1859 when Lyman Cutlar shot his neighbor's pig, the island was a functional but occasionally tense slice of western life.

The Belle Vue Sheep Farm on San Juan Island in October 1859, about a mile from where Lyman Cutlar shot Charles Griffin's pig. Although the sheep farm was established by the British-owned Hudson's Bay Company, a spot just north of this location became the site of the U.S. Army camp, and later of the permanent American Camp.

And you know the rest. After the shooting of the pig, events quickly escalated until the two nations hovered on the brink of war. The United States, marching darkly toward the bloody Civil War, had no desire to entangle itself in this conflict. As for the British, they had just come off a number of intense wars and skirmishes of their own in Europe and Asia. But both sides had their pride, and both warned that if the other side fired one shot, they would fire back.

There were many heroes in this almost-war. Notwithstanding the actions of a few hotheads, men of power checked their egos and even disobeyed commands in order to avoid bloodshed.

That peace was maintained, that weapons were laid down, that the two sides became neighbors and friends for the next thirteen years, was a miracle much bigger than the size of the island.

True, there were wrinkles. They bickered over ownership of limestone quarries. They played tricks on the law—if an American got in trouble, he'd pretend he was British, and if a Brit got in trouble, he'd pretend he was American. (What sneaks!) And sometimes they got confused about which side they belonged to—one British soldier deserted, then showed up later in an American uniform, putting the officials in a quandary about how to punish him.

But most of the time, things went swimmingly. Despite the presence of the two military camps, peace reigned, and in fact all artillery was prohibited. The Americans and British really did go to each other's parties, and no doubt they took tea (and sometimes stronger beverages) together. Did they teach each other baseball and cricket? Maybe. We don't know.

At English Camp, on the shores of placid Garrison Bay, the commander created a fine formal garden for his wife. A vegetable garden flourished. There was a fancy multilevel birdhouse, a summer house; there were concerts and theatricals. The Brits decorated for New Year's Day with holly and evergreen. The Yanks quite enjoyed visiting.

American Camp, at the opposite end of the island, was much cruder and more utilitarian, at least on a day-to-day basis. But the men there still hosted jolly gatherings. They put on picnics, dances, and fireworks.

Civilians (sometimes as many as 180 at a time) came by boat all the way from Victoria, on Vancouver Island, to join in the festivities at both camps. As you can imagine, the camps grew famous for their parties!

But all good things must come to an end, and in 1872 the two countries consulted an outside arbiter, Kaiser Wilhelm I of Germany, to determine ownership. (Another wise move. Sometimes an unbiased third party is the way to go. This is considered one of the earliest examples of international arbitration.) Kaiser Wilhelm ruled that the border should run just northwest of the San Juan Islands, placing them under American dominion. The islanders were notified by telegram. The British ships sailed out of Garrison Bay; two years later the American troops withdrew as well. Thus ended the last armed conflict between the two countries.

The British left with regret, both for the dignified, pleasant camp they had grown fond of and for their American friends. The Yanks, for their part, felt the loss of the high-spirited Brits after their departure.

Can countries share? These two did. Clear thinking, diplomacy, and restraint were their tools. Peace and civility were the result. In today's world, where nations fight bitter wars over boundary disputes and people must increasingly leave their homeland in search of safer shores, it is more important than ever that we learn to share our resources and to solve our problems peacefully.

Let us follow the example of the Pig War.

ABOVE: Royal Marines pose in the newly established English Camp, at the northern end of San Juan Island. The British remained at English Camp from 1860 until 1872, when the border conflict ended and the island was handed over to America. No artillery was allowed at either camp during this time of joint occupation.

LEFT: U.S. Army soldiers pose with a Napoleon gun sometime in October 1859, near the U.S. Army camp at the southern end of San Juan Island. At this point, both sides were poised for war. Happily, not a shot was ever fired, and the Pig War would end about two months later.

TIMELINE

1776–1781: The Americans clash with the British in the Revolutionary War and win their independence.

1818: After the War of 1812, the British and the Americans sign a treaty allowing for joint exploration and occupation of the Oregon Country.

1846: Lawmakers write the Oregon Treaty, which defines the boundary between the American and British territories as running west along the 49th parallel and then south through a channel between the British Vancouver Island and the American mainland.

1846–1859: The nationality of the San Juan Islands, which lie in the middle of the channel, remains undecided. A small number of Americans and British work and stake claims on San Juan Island.

1853: James Douglas, governor of the Crown Colonies of Vancouver Island and British Columbia, establishes the Belle Vue Sheep Farm on San Juan Island. Charles Griffin becomes the manager.

June 15, 1859: Lyman Cutlar shoots Charles Griffin's pig, triggering the San Juan Island Boundary Dispute, also known as the Pig War.

July 11, 1859: The Americans write to General William S. Harney, commander of the Department of Oregon, asking for military protection.

July 18, 1859: Harney orders Captain George E. Pickett to San Juan Island.

July 27, 1859: Pickett arrives on the island with sixty-four men, two 12-pound guns, and one 6-pound gun.

July 29, 1859: Governor James Douglas sends Captain Geoffrey Phipps Hornby, aboard the HMS *Tribune*, to San Juan Island with thirty-one guns. Two more ships, the *Satellite* and the *Plumper*, arrive shortly after. In total, the Brits now have sixty-four guns and close to nine hundred men.

July 30, 1859: Pickett requests reinforcements.

July 31, 1859: Hornby parleys with Pickett and asks Pickett to withdraw. Pickett refuses.

August 3, 1859: Hornby ignores Douglas's order to land troops on the island.

August 5, 1859: Rear Admiral R. Lambert Baynes, the Pacific Station commander, arrives. He is appalled by the situation but praises Hornby's actions.

August 10, 1859: Under the command of Lieutenant Colonel Silas Casey, 171 Americans arrive on the island. Casey assumes command from Pickett. American troops now number approximately 460.

September 3, 1859: On behalf of President James Buchanan, W. R. Drinkard, Acting Secretary of War, writes to General Harney expressing alarm at the escalation.

October 1859: Lieutenant General Winfield Scott arrives in the area, at the behest of President Buchanan but with the support of both sides, to negotiate the joint occupation.

1860–1872: A small number of American and British troops (fewer than one hundred on each side) jointly and peacefully occupy San Juan Island.

1861–1865: The Civil War ravages the United States.

October 21, 1872: The German emperor Kaiser Wilhelm I concludes arbitration. His commission decides that the boundary line between the British territories and the United States of America shall run through the Haro Strait, not the Rosario. Thus, San Juan Islands will lie under American dominion.

November 1872: All Royal Marines depart San Juan Island.

1874: American troops withdraw.

September 1966: An act of Congress creates the San Juan Island National Historical Park (also known as American and English Camps, San Juan Island).

RESOURCES

All quotations in the book can be found in the following sources marked with an asterisk (*).

PRIMARY SOURCES

Friday Harbor, (Washington), *San Juan Islander*, 1909.

*Howay, F. W., Lewis, William S., and Meyers, Jacob A., "Angus McDonald: A Few Items from the West." *Washington Historical Quarterly*, 8:3, (July 1917).

Hudson's Bay Company Records, microfilm, *Post Journals, Belle Vue Sheep Farm, 1854-1855 and 1858-1862.* Hudson's Bay Company Archives, Winnipeg, Manitoba, Canada.

*Macfie, Matthew. *Vancouver Island and British Columbia, their History, Resources and Prospects.* London: Longman, Green, 1865.

*McKay, Charles, "History of San Juan Island." *Washington Historical Quarterly*, 2:4, 1908.

Miller, David Hunter. *San Juan Archipelago: Study of the Joint Occupation of San Juan Island.* Bellows Falls, VT: Wyndham Press, 1943. (Note: This includes primary sources such as letters sent between military commanders.)

Post Records, San Juan Islands, volumes 1-7a.

Seattle, (Washington), *Post-Intelligencer*, 1892.

*Sprague, Roderick, Ed. *San Juan Archaeology.* Moscow, ID: University of Idaho, 1983.

*U.S. Congress. Senate. *Executive Document No. 29. 40th Congr., 2nd Sess. Report of the Secretary of State.* Washington City: 1867-1868.

FOR FURTHER READING

Coleman, E. C. *The Pig War: The Most Perfect War in History.* Stroud, UK: The History Press, 2009.

Holtzen, Mark. *The Pig War.* North Charleston, SC: CreateSpace, 2012.

Neering, Rosemary. *The Pig War: The Last Canada-US Border Conflict.* Victoria, BC: Heritage House Publishing, 2011.

Vouri, Mike. *The Pig War: Images of America.* Charleston, SC: Arcadia, 2008.

Vouri, Mike. *The Pig War: Standoff at Griffin Bay.* Seattle, WA: Discover Your Northwest, 2016 (first edition 1999).

WEBSITES*

modernfarmer.com/2014/03/inside-great-pig-war-1859

nps.gov/sajh/index.htm

thesanjuans.com

VISIT

San Juan is the second-largest and most populous island in the archipelago called the San Juan Islands. Located in the Pacific Northwest's Salish Sea, in between the United States and Canada, the archipelago consists of over four hundred islands in all, if you count the rocks that disappear at high tide. (Only 128 of the islands are named.) They are a popular tourist destination for people not only from the Pacific Northwest (western Oregon and Washington State) but from all over the world, and are enjoyed for their serene, natural beauty. You can get to the islands of San Juan, Orcas, Lopez, and Shaw by ferry. To access the others, visitors take charter boats or small airplanes.

ACKNOWLEDGMENTS

I want to extend huge thanks to Mike Vouri. As the longtime chief of interpretation and historian of the San Juan Island National Historical Park, he spent years researching the border dispute. The result, his authoritative scholarly books about the Pig War, were the foundation upon which I built my own book. Here, I have attempted to crystallize the peace-championing message of the dispute so that it can resonate for young readers. This book would not exist without Mike's previous efforts.

Thanks also to my editor, Carolyn Yoder; my agent, Essie White; my cousin, Michèle Ruess, who first suggested this topic; my mom, Sally Bland, who loved it; the wonderful illustrator, Alison Jay, who brought it all to life; and my talented critique partners, who supported me along the way—Ariel Bernstein, Ali Bovis, Katey Howes, Marta Lindsey, Kristin Mahoney, Victoria Sanchez, and Meredith Steiner.

ARTIST'S NOTE

In a nod to her British roots, Alison Jay named the pig K Edward (page 40) after a potato variety, King Edward, grown in the United Kingdom. The potato honors King Edward VII.

For Essie, who believed in me from the start. —EBS

To Claude and Lizzy,
thank you for being such wonderful neighbours,
if my pig escaped I'm sure you would let him eat your potatoes. —AJ

PICTURE CREDITS

National Park Service: 44-45

Yale Collection of Western Americana, Beinecke Rare Book and Manuscript Library: 43

Calkins Creek
An imprint of Astra Books for Young Readers, a division of Astra Publishing House
astrapublishinghouse.com
Printed in China

ISBN: 978-1-68437-171-6 (hc)
ISBN: 978-1-63592-451-0 (eBook)
Library of Congress Control Number: 2019953728

First edition
10 9 8 7 6 5 4 3 2

Design by Barbara Grzeslo
The text is set in Neutraface.
The illustrations are done with Alkyd paint on paper with a crackle glaze varnish.